Brittany F. Coburn

PRAY TOGETHER

A 6 week couples prayer guide

BRITTANY F. COBURN

WESTBOW
PRESS®
A DIVISION OF THOMAS NELSON
& ZONDERVAN

This book is a work of non-fiction. Unless otherwise noted, the author and the publisher make no explicit guarantees as to the accuracy of the information contained in this book and in some cases, names of people and places have been altered to protect their privacy.

WestBow Press books may be ordered through booksellers or by contacting:

WestBow Press
A Division of Thomas Nelson & Zondervan
1663 Liberty Drive
Bloomington, IN 47403
www.westbowpress.com
844-714-3454

Because of the dynamic nature of the Internet, any web addresses or links contained in this book may have changed since publication and may no longer be valid. The views expressed in this work are solely those of the author and do not necessarily reflect the views of the publisher, and the publisher hereby disclaims any responsibility for them.

Any people depicted in stock imagery provided by Getty Images are models, and such images are being used for illustrative purposes only.
Certain stock imagery © Getty Images.

Scripture quotations marked (ESV) are from The ESV® Bible (The Holy Bible, English Standard Version®), copyright © 2001 by Crossway, a publishing ministry of Good News Publishers. Used by permission. All rights reserved.

ISBN: 978-1-6642-6403-8 (sc)
ISBN: 978-1-6642-6404-5 (hc)
ISBN: 978-1-6642-6402-1 (e)

Library of Congress Control Number: 2022907207

Print information available on the last page.

WestBow Press rev. date: 05/25/2022

CONTENTS

For Christopher,
I know God loves me an infinite amount because
he gave me you. I love you more…

I am so glad that you are joining me on this journey as a couple. I wrote this daily prayer guide because I saw a need in my marriage and figured that we were not the only couple feeling the need for guided prayer time together.

I pray you use this to grow in the Lord together as a couple. The questions are there for you to be open and honest with each other, and to create a bond and intimacy through scripture and through talking out your fears, goals, desires, strengths, and weaknesses. Even though you are in a close relationship already, some of these questions might make you uncomfortable, but please make it a priority to be open and honest. Honesty is key to having long-lasting relationships with your significant others and with the Lord. I pray for you in this journey. I pray that you find blessings in all areas from the time that you spend with the Lord together. May this journey be one that you will look back on and see the hand of God guiding you together and changing who you were into who he desires you to be.

Dating Couples:

I want you to use this prayer guide to get to know each other better and to reflect on where the Lord is guiding you as a couple. I do *not* want you to use this to grow intimate in a way that is not Christ-centered. I would suggest that when you pray together, you do it away from anywhere that would lead to temptations. A significant other who desires the Lord over all other things is sexy. I get it. Be smart and pray together in an open space. But enjoy your time together in the Lord.

WEEK 1

Spiritual Growth

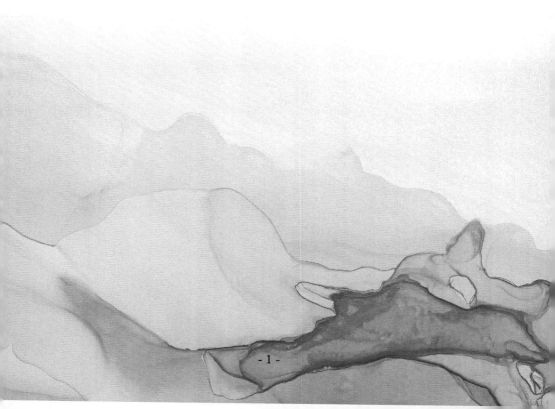

As you start out on this journey as a couple, I want you to focus on getting to know each other more. If you have been together for two weeks or together for fifty-five years, I am sure there are things that the Lord wants you to reveal to each other during this journey. But more importantly, there are areas where the Lord wants you to lean into him and grow closer to him. Your spiritual growth is of the utmost importance during your six weeks. We are not to stay in a comfortable spot, merely sit and listen to a sermon weekly, say a mediocre prayer over dinner, and check off a box or two. We are called to press in and grow in our walk with the Lord. The Holy Spirit is ready and wants to meet with you. He wants you to allow him to stretch and mold you into what you were made to be. When we have a significant other willing to press in and grow with us, it makes the journey so much more fulfilling. God is for marriage and relationships, and growing spiritually together is part of his plan.

This week, I want you to focus on what God is trying to teach you. The questions are written so that you will be open and honest with yourself, each other, and with the Lord. Go in with the mindset that you will share your heart with each other. Be honest. Embrace what could possibly be hard. During this journey, there may be moments that feel painful or awkward. You may not want to share the full truth. You may want to keep things hidden, or there may be things that you have even hidden from yourself, but the Lord wants to bring those to light. Spiritual growth can sometimes be painful and hard. But I can promise that when you allow the Lord to work in and through you and you are open and honest with everyone involved, it will end up being a beautiful journey that brings you closer to each other and to Christ.

To start off this journey, we are going to look at Psalm 139 over the course of the next five days. This chapter of Psalms is a beautiful picture of how we are not a mistake, and how everything was planned out about us before we even were. David's words beautifully encapsulate how the God of the universe feels about each of us. He wanted each and every one of us on this planet for a reason and for a purpose. He also wanted us to stretch and grow, and to fully walk in what he desires for us. When David prays "search me," he is setting an example of doing hard things, like putting in work on ourselves and not staying in our sinful brokenness. God wants us to be fully present, fully alive, and fully able to reach others about the gospel. If we are hiding from our significant other, from the Lord and/or from ourselves, we are not living out why we were created.

The good, and possibly frustrating news, is that we are never far from the presence of God. No matter where we go, God is there. We cannot hide. He knows us better than we know ourselves. He sees our ups and downs. He sees what we are trying to hide. He sees what we are trying to overcome on our own. He knows our fears and what brings us joy. We merely need to say, "Here I am Lord, search me. Show me what needs to change. Bring me closer to you and reveal where I need change." Let's take it a step further and pray the same thing but as a couple: "You see us. Make us pure. Reveal what needs to change in us and bring us closer to you, so that together, we can do mighty things in your name."

This week, may you find strength to pray hard prayers. May you grow closer to Christ and each other. By the end of this first week, my hope is that you walk away knowing more of who you are, and knowing that you belong and that you are loved by God and each other. May this journey be one of beauty and growth.

DAY 1

Scripture: Psalm 139:1–4

You have searched me, Lord,
and you know me.
You know when I sit and when I rise;
you perceive my thoughts from afar.
You discern my going out and my lying down;
you are familiar with all my ways.
Before a word is on my tongue
you, Lord, know it completely.

DAY 1

1. What is your first reaction to knowing that God is fully aware of every one of your thoughts, words, and motives?

2. What is an area you feel God is examining and bringing to your attention?

3. How can you apply the knowledge that God knows your every thought and action to draw you closer to him?

DAY 1

Lord,

We know that your word says that you know our every thought and motive before we do. Please make us aware that you are always observing and listening—not to scare us or intimidate us into obedience, but to help us realize you are there to lead, guide, and love us. We give you complete control over our thoughts. Make us aware when these things do not line up with your scripture or your view of the world. Create in us pure hearts and minds so that we may be worthy of being called your children.

In Jesus's name,

Amen

We are grateful for...

1.

2.

3.

Prayer Requests

O

O

O

O

O

O

O

O

O

O

DAY 2

Scripture: Psalm 139:5–10

You hem me in, behind and before, and lay your hand upon me. Such knowledge is too wonderful for me; it is high; I cannot attain it.
Where shall I go from your Spirit? Or where shall I flee from your presence?
If I ascend to heaven, you are there! If I make my bed in Sheol, you are there!
If I take the wings of the morning and dwell in the uttermost parts of the sea,
even there your hand shall lead me, and your right hand shall hold me.

DAY 2

1. Does it fill you with comfort or fear that you can never escape God?

2. Do you find yourself trying to run away from or draw closer to his presence? Why?

3. These verses prove that God is always there, ready to lead, guide, comfort, and sustain us. How do you need his presence in this moment of your life?

DAY 2

Lord,

Thank you that we cannot ever escape you. Though there are times we want to hide out in shame, you love us enough to never take your hand away from guiding us. Please help lead us into running to you in all circumstances. Help us to continually seek out your presence. May we find comfort and peace in the fact that we cannot escape your spirit.

In Jesus's name,

Amen

We are grateful for...

1.

2.

3.

Prayer Requests

○ _____

○ _____

○ _____

○ _____

○ _____

○ _____

○ _____

○ _____

○ _____

○ _____

DAY 3

Scripture: Psalm 139:11–12

If I say, "Surely the darkness shall cover me, and the light about me be night,"
even the darkness is not dark to you; the night is bright as the day,
for darkness is as light with you.

DAY 3

1. Scripture continually speaks about the light overcoming the darkness (e.g., John 1:5, John 8:12). How does it make you feel knowing the darkness cannot win?

2. What does it mean to you when scripture says that we cannot hide in darkness because dark and light are the same to God?

3. Do you have a dark place in your life that Christ needs to break through and shine his light on?

DAY 3

Lord,

Thank you that we cannot hide in the dark. We are grateful that you always see us and make us aware of your presence. Help us not to be fearful of our inability to hide in the darkness from you. Open our eyes to what a gift it is to be able to walk in your light. You want to know us and you seek us out even in our darkest places. Shine your light in the darkness and reveal where you need to take control. We give you our broken areas and ask you to heal them with your truth and with your light.

In Jesus's name,

Amen

We are grateful for...

1.

2.

3.

Prayer Requests

○

○

○

○

○

○

○

○

○

○

DAY 4

Scripture: Psalm 139:13–18

For you formed my inward parts; you knitted me together in my mother's womb.

I praise you, for I am fearfully and wonderfully made. Wonderful are your works;

my soul knows it very well. My frame was not hidden from you, when I was being made in secret, intricately woven in the depths of the earth.

Your eyes saw my unformed substance; in your book were written, every one of them, the days that were formed for me, when as yet there was none of them.

How precious to me are your thoughts, O God! How vast is the sum of them!

If I would count them, they are more than the sand. I awake, and I am still with you.

DAY 4

1. Have you ever thought that you were a complete mistake or any part of you was a mistake?

2. How do you think God's thoughts about you differ from others' thoughts about you? How do his thoughts differ from your thoughts about yourself?

3. If you knew the exact amount of days you had left on this earth, would you live your life differently?

DAY 4

Lord,

You created us wholly and perfectly. There are no mistakes to be found in us. Thank you for the care and precision you put into creating every detail of our looks, personalities, interests, and thoughts. Help us to offer ourselves back to you as living sacrifices. Help us to not waste a single day, but to walk in your love with everyone we come in contact with. Help the way we treat each other be a reflection of you. May your name be glorified in your creation. May we walk in the knowledge of your thoughts toward us.

In Jesus's name,

Amen

We are grateful for…

1.

2.

3.

Prayer Requests

O

O

O

O

O

O

O

O

O

O

DAY 5

Scripture: Psalm 139:19–24

Oh that you would slay the wicked, O God!

O men of blood, depart from me!

They speak against you with malicious intent; your enemies take your name in vain.

Do I not hate those who hate you, O Lord?

And do I not loathe those who rise up against you? I hate them with complete hatred; I count them my enemies.

Search me, O God, and know my heart!

Try me and know my thoughts! And see if there be any grievous way in me, and lead me in the way everlasting!

DAY 5

1. Is your relationship with Christ one that would make you feel the same hatred that David felt towards those who hated Christ?

2. Does the thought of praying the prayer in verses 23 and 24 scare you? Why or why not?

3. If you truly prayed and meant this prayer, would you be willing to change things the Holy Spirit opened your eyes to?

DAY 5

Lord,

Just as David prayed, we ask you to examine us. Search our hearts and see if there are any idolatrous tendencies in us. Then please walk with us as we change to be more like you. We cannot do any of this on our own. Our human nature is built to fail, but you do not fail. We know you are living and working inside of us because we are your sons and daughters. Please help us to resemble more of you and less of our human nature in our personal lives and in our relationship as a couple. Thank you for your help in all areas.

In Jesus's name,

Amen

We are grateful for...

1.

2.

3.

Prayer Requests

○

○

○

○

○

○

○

○

○

○

WEEK 2

Relationships

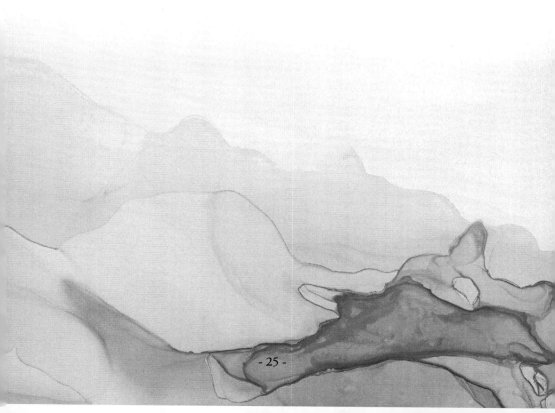

Relationships come in all shapes and sizes. There are those we are born with: parents, siblings, grandparents, aunts, uncles, and more. Then there are the ones we choose: friends, significant others, those we really don't like, and those we have to pretend to like. There are spiritual relationships and our relationship with Christ himself. No matter what type of relationship, there will be times of joy, times of anger and frustration, and times you just want to end it all and start over with someone else.

God has called us to love and to be loved by those around us. He created us for community, because we are better together than we are apart. Our relationships with our significant others are important because they are who we choose to live our lives with. We should be running on the same mission and supporting each other in our callings. Your first focus this week should be to make sure each of you is on the same page in your relationship. If you are married, set out to evaluate your relationship with each other and with Christ. What areas do you need to work on so that you both are pulling your weight in supporting each other? How can you show the other that you are in this, and desire to grow closer to Christ as a couple? If you are dating, what needs to happen to make your relationship look like one that God is a part of and guiding? Do you both have a proper understanding of how God fits and moves in a relationship? Spend time talking about marriage and how it would look for you to move in that direction with Christ as the center, guiding and leading you both.

Do not merely focus on your romantic relationship. Branch out and apply the questions and scriptures to your friendships, and family, work, and church relationships. Each and every person that you are in some sort of relationship with is there for a reason. God found it necessary to put that person in your life. You may be the only Jesus that person sees. Maybe that person needs to feel loved and accepted by someone and you are that someone. There may be difficult relationships that you can learn from or relationships that you need to be the bigger person in. Wherever you find yourselves in relationships, you need to be allowing the Holy Spirit to work and move through you so that you are a representation of Christ himself.

The world tells us that we need to make the relationship about us. If we aren't getting our needs met or we walk away not feeling fulfilled, then it is perfectly fine to cut the other person out and move on. However, Christ tells us that we are supposed to be examples of love. We need to be patient, kind, and supportive. Our words need to be words of building up and not tearing down. Sometimes, this can be super easy, and other times it will be the hardest thing we will face at that moment. Whatever the situation, God has called you to love and be loved. You need to stretch yourself and see how you can improve to be the best possible person to be in a relationship. This does not mean being the best possible person on our own merit. We must show the love of Christ in such a way that people walk away from us changed for the better. You can do it. Together you can discuss how you view your personal relationship and how you view your relationships with others. What are you putting into them and how much are you expecting to take away? Let the Holy Spirit speak and poke and prod. Become the best possible version of a friend, brother, sister, and mate that you possibly can become by allowing the Holy Spirit to work through you.

DAY 1

Scripture: Ephesians 5:22–29, 33

Wives, submit to your own husbands, as to the Lord. For the husband is the head of the wife even as Christ is the head of the church, his body, and is himself its Savior. Now as the church submits to Christ, so also wives should submit in everything to their husbands. Husbands, love your wives, as Christ loved the church and gave himself up for her, that he might sanctify her, having cleansed her by the washing of water with the word, so that he might present the church to himself in splendor, without spot or wrinkle or any such thing, that she might be holy and without blemish. In the same way husbands should love their wives as their own bodies. He who loves his wife loves himself. For no one ever hated his own flesh, but nourishes and cherishes it, just as Christ does the church, However, let each one of you love his wife as himself, and let the wife see that she respects her husband.

DAY 1

1. What does this passage tell you about the marriage relationship?

2. Biblical marriage is a reflection of Christ and his love for his children. What areas of your relationship could reflect Christ better?

3. Are the areas of submitting, respect, and/or love hard for you? If so, why?

DAY 1

Lord,

You set such a grand example for us in how you love your people. Help us to live out our marriage as a reflection of you. If there are areas where we struggle to love, respect, submit, or serve one another, point them out and then help us to correct them through your guidance. We desire our marriage to be an example of your love for the church. Use us to share the gospel through the way we love and serve once another.

In Jesus's name,

Amen

We are grateful for...

1.

2.

3.

Prayer Requests

○ _____

○ _____

○ _____

○ _____

○ _____

○ _____

○ _____

○ _____

○ _____

○ _____

DAY 2

Scripture: 1 Corinthians 13:4–7

Love is patient and kind; love does not envy or boast; it is not arrogant or rude.
It does not insist on its own way; it is not irritable or resentful; it does not rejoice at wrongdoing,
but rejoices with the truth.
Love bears all things, believes all things, hopes all things, endures all things.

DAY 2

1. Can you put your name in the place of love and feel confident it applies when talking about your marriage?

2. What about your other relationships?

3. Who comes to mind when you think of this verse? Why does that person come to mind first?

DAY 2

Lord,

Thank you for loving us and being the perfect example of how to love others. We know there are areas that we need to work on in order to love our significant other and those around us better. Please reveal to us how we can love our significant other the way that you love us. Show us the areas that we are not showing love to those around us, and also open our eyes to how to love you with our whole heart. We know that we will fail. We love because you first loved us, and we desire to love those around us with a Christ like love.

In Jesus's name,

Amen

We are grateful for...

1.

2.

3.

Prayer Requests

O

O

O

O

O

O

O

O

O

O

DAY 3

Scripture: Philippians 2:1–5

So if there is any encouragement in Christ, any comfort from love, any participation in the Spirit, any affection and sympathy, complete my joy by being of the same mind, having the same love, being in full accord and of one mind.

Do nothing from selfish ambition or conceit, but in humility count others more significant than yourselves. Let each of you look not only to his own interests, but also to the interests of others. Have this mind among yourselves, which is yours in Christ Jesus,

DAY 3

1. Do you find you have the same mind, goals, and love as your significant other? What about those around you?

2. Are you motivated by selfish ambition or humility? Be honest!

3. How can you be more intentional in pouring into the care and interests of your significant other? Others?

DAY 3

Lord,

Our human nature is to think only of ourselves and to take care of only our needs. Your word calls us to more. You have called us to love well, to be unified, and to care about others' interests and needs. Please show us how we can improve in our love towards others. Make us more aware of those around us and their interests and needs. We want to be better and love well. We desire for our relationships to flourish because you are at the center of each of them, and most importantly at the center of our lives.

In Jesus's name,

Amen

We are grateful for...

1.

2.

3.

Prayer Requests

○ _____

○ _____

○ _____

○ _____

○ _____

○ _____

○ _____

○ _____

○ _____

○ _____

DAY 4

Scripture: Proverbs 4:11–15, 19–23

I have taught you the way of wisdom; I have led you in the paths of uprightness.

When you walk, your step will not be hampered, and if you run, you will not stumble. Keep hold of instruction; do not let go; guard her, for she is your life. Do not enter the path of the wicked, and do not walk in the way of the evil.

Avoid it; do not go on it; turn away from it and pass on.

The way of the wicked is like deep darkness; they do not know over what they stumble.

My son, be attentive to my words; incline your ear to my sayings. Let them not escape from your sight; keep them within your heart.

For they are life to those who find them, and healing to all their flesh. Keep your heart with all vigilance, for from it flow the springs of life.

DAY 4

1. Who or what has the most influence over your life and decisions?

2. What are you doing to guard your heart? How can you do a better job?

3. How much influence do you allow the Holy Spirit to have in your day to day?

DAY 4

Lord,

We recognize there are people and things outside of you and your Holy Spirit that have influence over us. We repent for following their word over yours. Open our eyes to the influences that need to change in our lives and guide us by the power of your Holy Spirit. Allow us to be used as godly influences for our significant others and those around us. Help us to guard our hearts and to lean into you in all things.

In Jesus's name,

Amen

We are grateful for...

1.

2.

3.

Prayer Requests

○

○

○

○

○

○

○

○

○

○

DAY 5

Scripture: Ephesians 4:29–32

Let no corrupting talk come out of your mouths,
but only such as is good for building up, as fits the occasion, that it may give grace to those who hear. And do not grieve the Holy Spirit of God, by whom you were sealed for the day of redemption.
Let all bitterness and wrath and anger and clamor and slander be put away from you, along with all malice. Be kind to one another, tenderhearted, forgiving one another, as God in Christ forgave you.

DAY 5

1. Is your speech towards one another compassionate and forgiving? Or is it full of bitterness, anger, and quarreling?

2. How is your speech towards those outside of your family? What about when they aren't around?

3. How can you change your speech toward those in your home and those you are in relationship with outside your home?

DAY 5

Lord,

Your word says that our tongue has the power of life and death. We can speak life into our significant other or we can tear the person down. Make us aware of our speech and even our tone toward one another. May we speak life. May we be encouraging and loving, and not bitter and quarrelsome. Concerning those outside of our home, open our eyes to how we speak to them and speak about them. How we speak changes our perspective and the perspective of others. Guide our words to be life-giving and not deadly. Help us to see others and to speak about them the way you do.

In Jesus's name,

Amen

We are grateful for...

1.

2.

3.

Prayer Requests

O

O

O

O

O

O

O

O

O

O

WEEK 3

Finances

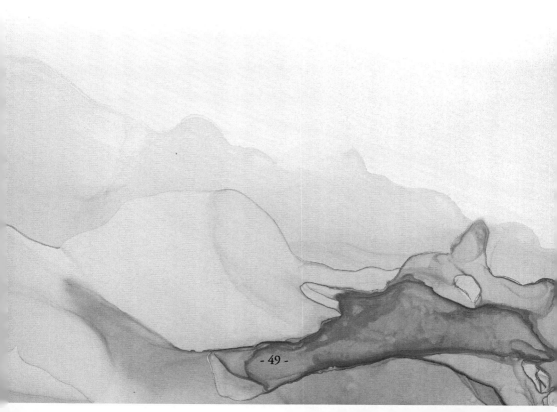

Everyone has an opinion on money, whether we verbally state it or not. We all know how we want to spend our money, and we definitely know how we are obtaining money. It costs to live and to survive. We are required to work to obtain food, and this is a scriptural requirement. Spiritually, how we view our finances, and what we do with them matters. We are called to give and called to be good stewards.

This next week, you are going to take a look at what scripture says about your finances and ask yourselves some questions concerning your mindset on money. Be honest with yourself and with your significant other. You may find that you are both on completely different pages when it comes to finances, and you may require time outside of this guide to talk about how you can get on the same page. One of you may really like to save while the other spends. In this case, how can you both come together to spend or save in a way that is life-giving for the other and also glorifies God in the process? In what ways do you both need to learn to honor God in your finances? In what ways do you need to give God the credit for all that you have?

Many times, the world says that you need to get more and that you deserve more. You work hard and you should be able to spend and play and do whatever you want with your finances. However, all that you have comes from the Lord. The doors opened for you to get the job you have because the Lord was guiding and directing you. He blesses by giving and he also takes away. He deserves all the credit for what we have. Are you giving him credit?

Not only does the world want all the credit for your success, but it also tells you to make it your identity. It says that you are what you have: the big house, the nice car, the nice clothing, the school your kids attend or will attend in the future. It is easy to get wrapped up in how you financially appear to outsiders and completely miss out on the blessings the Lord is preparing for you so your finances are honoring to him.

What is motivating you with giving and receiving? Does the world play a part in how you live your life financially? If so, there may be a lot of evaluating that needs to take place when it comes to your mindset on finances. It is also helpful for you and your significant other to be on the same page. So many relationships end, or are unhealthy, because of finances. Satan loves to use money to make or break people and relationships. It is one of the easiest idols for us to acquire without even really knowing it. I ask that this week, you each take a deep breath, and ask the Lord to really speak to you when it comes to your heart and money. Then hold hands and deep dive into finding out what the Holy Spirit wants to say to you when it comes to your finances and your mindset. You may just walk away feeling more free after this week, if you both allow the Holy Spirit to move and change some things in you. Let him do the work, and rest knowing that he gives and takes away where he sees fit for our good and his glory.

DAY 1

Scripture: James 1:17 and Romans 11:33–36

Every good gift and every perfect gift is from above, coming down from the Father of lights, with whom there is no variation or shadow due to change. (James 1:17)

Oh, the depth of the riches and wisdom and knowledge of God! How unsearchable are his judgments and how inscrutable his ways! "For who has known the mind of the Lord, or who has been his counselor?" "Or who has given a gift to him that he might be repaid?" For from him and through him and to him are all things. To him be glory forever. Amen. (Romans 11:33–36)

DAY 1

1. Do you see your financial status as something you achieved, as a gift from God, or as your own hot mess?

2. Do you recognize all you have (material and financial) as a gift from the Lord or as a result of your own hard work and determination?

3. God does not owe us anything, and what we have is a generous gift from our heavenly father. How can you worship, from a heart of gratitude, using what you have been given?

DAY 1

Lord,

Thank you for loving us enough to give us good gifts. We lack nothing because you take care of our needs in every way. You are so generous with your gifts and we do not deserve them. Thank you for your love, your care, and your attention to the smallest details. Help us to not take anything we have for granted. Open our eyes to your goodness when we fail to see it. Help us to worship you with all that you have given us. We love you and again, we thank you for your generous love towards us and all the many blessings that we have on a daily basis. May we recognize your hand in all that we have and all that we are given.

In Jesus's name,

Amen

We are grateful for...

1.

2.

3.

Prayer Requests

O

O

O

O

O

O

O

O

O

O

DAY 2

Scripture: Proverbs 15:27, 15:6, and Luke 12:15

Whoever is greedy for unjust gain troubles his own household, but he who hates bribes will live. (Proverbs 15:27)

In the house of the righteous there is much treasure, but trouble befalls the income of the wicked. (Proverbs 15:6)

And he said to them, "Take care, and be on your guard against all covetousness, for one's life does not consist in the abundance of his possessions." (Luke 12:15)

DAY 2

1. What is your true motivation for earning and spending money?

2. Greed tends to be followed closely by trouble. Are there any areas that the Holy Spirit might be pointing out greed before trouble comes?

3. Does your financial status bring an air of entitlement? Do you say to yourself, *I have nothing so I deserve this*? Or do you say to yourself, *I work hard and I am owed this*?

DAY 2

Lord,

We repent for any time we have come across as greedy or entitled. These mindsets are not of you. You desire for us to give from a joyful heart and to live with open hands. Please point out any areas where we tend to let greed or entitlement control our words or actions. Forgive us for putting finances and the gain of material possessions before you. We want to recognize that all we have is a gift from you. Open our eyes to how blessed we are, with and without wealth and material things, not because of our own initiative but because you give good gifts to your children.

In Jesus's name,

Amen

We are grateful for...

1.

2.

3.

Prayer Requests

○

○

○

○

○

○

○

○

○

○

DAY 3

Scripture: 2 Corinthians 9:6–11

The point is this: whoever sows sparingly will also reap sparingly, and whoever sows bountifully will also reap bountifully. Each one must give as he has decided in his heart, not reluctantly or under compulsion, for God loves a cheerful giver. And God is able to make all grace abound to you, so that having all sufficiency in all things at all times, you may abound in every good work. As it is written, "He has distributed freely, he has given to the poor; his righteousness endures forever." He who supplies seed to the sower and bread for food will supply and multiply your seed for sowing and increase the harvest of your righteousness. You will be enriched in every way to be generous in every way, which through us will produce thanksgiving to God.

DAY 3

1. After taking a few minutes to honestly evaluate your heart, do you find that you are a generous giver or do you find giving hard?

2. Do you find that you give out of joy, reluctance, or compulsion?

3. How can you and the Holy Spirit work together to give more generously from a joyful heart?

DAY 3

Lord,

Your word calls us to be generous givers. We recognize that at different times, due to different circumstances, we have been tight-fisted with what we have been blessed with. Change our hearts to be more like yours, and teach us to not only give, but to do so with joyful hearts. Help us to not give from a place of reluctance or a place of compulsion, but to give after thinking about and praying over our gift. Open our eyes to the needs of others while also giving us your wisdom to guide and direct us.

In Jesus's name,

Amen

We are grateful for...

1.

2.

3.

Prayer Requests

○

○

○

○

○

○

○

○

○

○

DAY 4

Scripture: Philippians 4:11–13 and Matthew 6:25–26

Not that I am speaking of being in need, for I have learned in whatever situation I am to be content. I know how to be brought low, and I know how to abound. In any and every circumstance, I have learned the secret of facing plenty and hunger, abundance and need. I can do all things through him who strengthens me.
(Philippians 4:11–13)

Therefore I tell you, do not be anxious about your life, what you will eat or what you will drink, nor about your body, what you will put on. Is not life more than food, and the body more than clothing? Look at the birds of the air: they neither sow nor reap nor gather into barns, and yet your heavenly Father feeds them. Are you not of more value than they?
(Matthew 6:25–26)

DAY 4

1. Do you have trouble believing that God will supply all of your needs? Why or why not?

2. Do you find yourself taking on the responsibility of supplying in abundance for your family? If so, why do you feel this is a need?

3. In what way can the Holy Spirit speak into this area in order for you to trust him fully?

DAY 4

Lord,

Thank you for being our provider in all things. Make us more aware of the ways you have provided in the past, and also keep us aware of your provisions from this moment forward. When we start taking responsibility for providing all things for our household, and stress or pride starts to develop, remind us that all responsibility belongs to you. Give us the strength to hand it all back to you. Give us peace in knowing that you are the ultimate provider. We desire for all of our trust to be in you. We believe if you provide for the birds, you will provide more for your children. Thank you that we can put our trust fully in you.

In Jesus's name,

Amen

We are grateful for...

1.

2.

3.

Prayer Requests

O

O

O

O

O

O

O

O

O

O

DAY 5

Scripture: Proverbs 3:9–10, Malachi 3:10, and Luke 6:38

Honor the Lord with your wealth and with the first-fruits of all your produce; then your barns will be filled with plenty, and your vats will be bursting with wine.
(Proverbs 3:9–10)

Bring the full tithe into the storehouse, that there may be food in my house. And thereby put me to the test, says the Lord of hosts, if I will not open the windows of heaven for you and pour down for you a blessing until there is no more need.
(Malachi 3:10)

Bring the full tithe into the storehouse, that there may be food in my house. And thereby put me to the test, says the Lord of hosts, if I will not open the windows of heaven for you and pour down for you a blessing until there is no more need.
(Malachi 3:10)

DAY 5

1. Is tithing and giving back to God something you practice regularly?

2. How have you seen God bless you after you have given back to him?

3. In what ways can you improve your giving and/or your attitude on giving?

DAY 5

Lord,

We have because you are generous with your children. Thank you for blessing us in the ways that you have. Please bring awareness to the fact that all that we have first belonged to you. You told the leaders to give to Caesar what belonged to Caesar and to God what belonged to God. Help us to realize the impact that giving from our first fruits has on not just the blessings we receive but also on our hearts and spiritual lives. We desire to do your will and to draw closer to you. When that happens, we ask that you give us a generous spirit and open hands. Forgive us for anytime we have been close-fisted and open our eyes to areas that we may still be that way. Thank you for loving us enough to take time to shape and guide us in our giving.

In Jesus's name,

Amen

We are grateful for...

1.

2.

3.

Prayer Requests

○

○

○

○

○

○

○

○

○

○

WEEK 4

Sphere of Influence

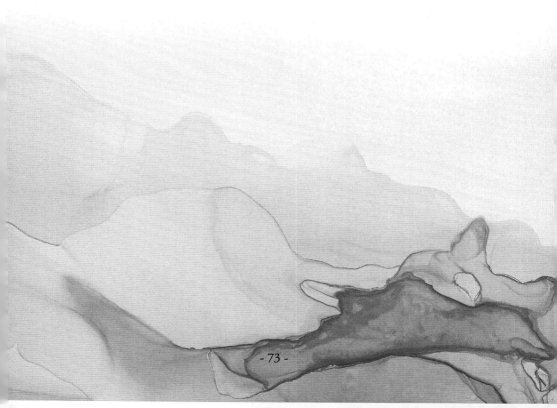

Do you realize that no matter who you are, where you work, or what your hobbies are, you have influence? There is always someone looking at you and wanting to either pattern a part of his or her life after yours, or maybe even the opposite. You may be struggling in an area and it shows, and those watching do not want to struggle in the same way. My point is that you are being watched and you have influence. How you use that influence matters not only to those watching but also, and more importantly, to the kingdom.

How you live, speak, and use your time and talents matters to how others view you, and shapes their opinion of Christ. If you share that you attend church, or that you are a Christian, people are watching to see if you will mess up and if you are a man or woman of your word. Do you act in a manner worthy of the gospel when people are watching, and when they are not?

Let's face it: you are going to fail in front of people because you are a sinner saved by grace. It's how you handle failure that matters. You need to be a person of your word and you need to have a repentant heart. The Bible says to be in the world and not of the world, and it's a hard and fine line to follow. You need to be a high level of influence on those you are surrounded by without being influenced by their sinful natures. It's easy to slip into becoming multiple versions of yourself: the church version and the worldly version. This is a dangerous and slippery slope because of how people are watching. Your goal should be to influence everyone you encounter by your consistency. Be the same person to the coworker who uses foul language and talks about inappropriate things as you would be to the sweet old lady at church who loves Jesus with everything inside her. When you are all things to all people, those who truly know you will see your walk as a joke. It's harsh to hear, but that is the reality of what is happening every day while you walk the planet. You are either an example of Christ's love or a moral joke.

You are an influence personally and also in your romantic relationship. How you talk about your significant other when he or she is not around shows others what a Christian relationship is supposed to look like or not look like. As Christians, you need to show that there is hope for dating and marriage, especially in a world that wants to change how we look at marriage and ask if we really even need it. Marriage, when the Holy Spirit is involved and invited to function openly, is a beautiful and wonderful example of Christ's love for the church. Your goal should be to make your relationship such that people cannot deny the power of the Holy Spirit and the love that our savior has for his people. It is possible, even if you do not feel like it is at this moment.

This week, ask the Holy Spirit to reveal how you are viewed as a person. Ask yourself and each other the questions and see how the spirit moves you to change. Journal what he is speaking, and determine to take small steps in your day to be a positive and godly influence to every single person you come in contact with. If you struggle with being a negative influence, the impact that you will have when the spirit takes control and starts moving you to act and be different will be profound. There is no lost cause when it comes to the power of Christ. You can be a gospel influence no matter what you look like in this moment. I pray this week that you realize how important you truly are and how much your voice and your actions matter to the kingdom.

DAY 1

Scripture: Titus 2:7–8, 11–13, 15

Show yourself in all respects to be a model of good works, and in your teaching show integrity, dignity, and sound speech that cannot be condemned, so that an opponent may be put to shame, having nothing evil to say about us. For the grace of God has appeared, bringing salvation for all people, training us to renounce ungodliness and worldly passions, and to live self-controlled, upright, and godly lives in the present age, waiting for our blessed hope, the appearing of the glory of our great God and Savior Jesus Christ, Declare these things; exhort and rebuke with all authority. Let no one disregard you.

DAY 1

1. Do you live your life in such a way that your opponents, or those around you, have nothing evil to say about you?

2. Do you see the importance of renouncing ungodliness and living a self-controlled, upright, and godly life?

3. How are you living out integrity, dignity, and sound speech? In what ways can you do better?

DAY 1

Lord,

You have laid out in your word what the Christ follower should look like to those around us. Due to our human and sinful nature, we fail daily. But you are living within us. Help those around us not to be influenced by our human actions, but, show them the Holy Spirit working in us. Help us to be a model of good works, full of integrity, dignity, and sound speech. Have us walk away from every situation leaving nothing bad to be said about us. We want you to be the main source of influence working through us and not our human and worldly desires. We truly desire for your name to be glorified above our names.

In Jesus's name,

Amen

We are grateful for...

1.

2.

3.

Prayer Requests

O _____

O _____

O _____

O _____

O _____

O _____

O _____

O _____

O _____

O _____

DAY 2

Scripture: Philippians 3:13–17

Brothers, I do not consider that I have made it my own. But one thing I do: forgetting what lies behind and straining forward to what lies ahead, I press on toward the goal for the prize of the upward call of God in Christ Jesus. Let those of us who are mature think this way, and if in anything you think otherwise, God will reveal that also to you. Only let us hold true to what we have attained. Brothers, join in imitating me, and keep your eyes on those who walk according to the example you have in us.

DAY 2

1. When you think of where you are in life, do your actions declare that it is because of God or because of you?

2. Are you constantly asking God to reveal to you where your thinking is not the same as his? If no, what is keeping you from asking?

3. Can you, with good conscience, tell others to imitate you the same way Paul did? Are there areas that require change first?

DAY 2

Lord,

You are a gracious and merciful God. We are who we are because of you. We cannot boast in ourselves but only in you. We have influence only because you have put us in that position. Help us to not waste any opportunities but to live worthy of our calling. Let us hold true to what we have attained. Show us ways that our thoughts are not your thoughts and help us to change our ways of thinking to match yours. We desire to be able to say "join in imitating me." But only by your grace and your help can that happen. We do not want to boast in ourselves but only in you.

In Jesus's name,

Amen

We are grateful for...

1.

2.

3.

Prayer Requests

O _____

O _____

O _____

O _____

O _____

O _____

O _____

O _____

O _____

O _____

DAY 3

Scripture: Romans 8:12–17

So then, brothers, we are debtors, not to the flesh, to live according to the flesh. For if you live according to the flesh you will die, but if by the Spirit you put to death the deeds of the body, you will live. For all who are led by the Spirit of God are sons of God. For you did not receive the spirit of slavery to fall back into fear, but you have received the Spirit of adoption as sons, by whom we cry, "Abba! Father!" The Spirit himself bears witness with our spirit that we are children of God, and if children, then heirs—heirs of God and fellow heirs with Christ, provided we suffer with him in order that we may also be glorified with him.

DAY 3

1. Do you find yourself being led by the spirit or the flesh more?

2. How can you lean more into your role as son or daughter of God and walk out of being fearful?

3. How can you use the fact that you are heirs of Christ to influence those around you?

DAY 3

Lord,

You have called us sons and daughters from the moment we accepted you as Lord of our lives. Fear and the world tend to make us forget our titles as heirs to Christ. Please help us to focus on our titles and calling, so that we may better influence those around us. We know that when we walk with our heads held high, no matter what comes our way, we are heirs, and people notice. Help our confidence in being your children not to falter but to draw attention to our relationship with you. Keep our eyes on the goal of being witnesses through our speech and actions. This is only possible with your help.

In Jesus's name,

Amen

We are grateful for...

1.

2.

3.

Prayer Requests

○

○

○

○

○

○

○

○

○

○

DAY 4

Scripture: Colossians 4:5–6, Matthew 5:13–16

Walk in wisdom toward outsiders, making the best use of the time. Let your speech always be gracious, seasoned with salt, so that you may know how you ought to answer each person.
(Colossians 4:5–6)

"You are the salt of the earth, but if salt has lost its taste, how shall its saltiness be restored? It is no longer good for anything except to be thrown out and trampled under people's feet. Nor do people light a lamp and put it under a basket, but on a stand, and it gives light to all in the house. You are the light of the world. A city set on a hill cannot be hidden. In the same way, let your light shine before others, so that they may see your good works and give glory to your Father who is in heaven."
(Matthew 5:13–16)

DAY 4

1. As a couple, how are you being salt and light to those around you? What about individually?

2. Have you ever struggled with the feeling that you were losing your saltiness or that your light was being covered up? How did you fight it?

3. How do you feel God calling you to add salt and light to your sphere of influence?

DAY 4

Lord,

You have given us the power to add godly flavor to our world. You have asked us to use our love for you to shed light into the darkness of our world. There have been so many times when we have failed, but you are always providing opportunities for us to do your work. Help us to see areas where we have lost our saltiness and where we need to work on projecting your light more effectively. We want to change your world by the power you have placed within us. Give us eyes to see and ears to hear. Open our eyes to the areas that need your salt and your light. Help us to always be aware of the sphere of influence that we have.

In Jesus's name,

Amen

We are grateful for...

1.

2.

3.

Prayer Requests

○ _____

○ _____

○ _____

○ _____

○ _____

○ _____

○ _____

○ _____

○ _____

○ _____

DAY 5

Scripture: 2 Corinthians 10:13–18

But we will not boast beyond limits, but will boast only with regard to the area of influence God assigned to us, to reach even to you. For we are not overextending ourselves, as though we did not reach you. For we were the first to come all the way to you with the gospel of Christ. We do not boast beyond limit in the labors of others. But our hope is that as your faith increases, our area of influence among you may be greatly enlarged, so that we may preach the gospel in lands beyond you, without boasting of work already done in another's area of influence. "Let the one who boasts, boast in the Lord." For it is not the one who commends himself who is approved, but the one whom the Lord commends.
(2 Corinthians 10:13–18)

DAY 5

1. Do you try to overextend the sphere of influence assigned to you or do you try to minimize it?

2. Does the thought that you have way more influence than you probably realize excite or scare you? Why?

3. We do not need to compete with others for influence. Instead, we must work with what Holy Spirit has given us and pray for expanse. How can you pray for those in your sphere? How do you see your sphere expanding?

DAY 5

Lord,

The influence we have is due to what you have given us. May we not try to shrink it or expand it, especially on our own human terms and conditions. You are who opens and closes eyes and hearts, and we are merely vessels working to plant seeds. Help us to realize that each word spoken, whether to each other or those around us, is influential. You have given us the power to influence people towards the gospel in a positive or negative light. Each person we talk to forms an opinion on who we are and who you are through our words and actions. Bring this to mind constantly so that we never let our guard down. May we always set a positive example of who you are.

In Jesus's name,

Amen

We are grateful for...

1.

2.

3.

Prayer Requests

○ _____

○ _____

○ _____

○ _____

○ _____

○ _____

○ _____

○ _____

○ _____

○ _____

WEEK 5

Worship

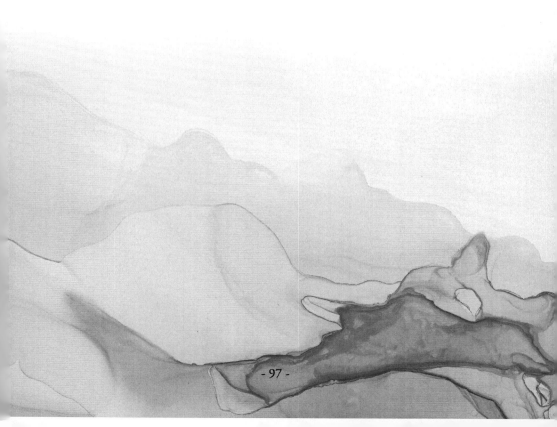

When I say that we will be discussing worship this week, I am not just talking about standing together in a church service singing a bunch of songs. That is one of my favorite ways to worship, as music flows through my veins. Every single part of our lives is made to worship the Lord. How we speak, how we move, and what we eat can all be forms of worship, when we put our intentions in the correct space.

I have always loved worship music. My dad was a worship leader while I was growing up, and I was taught to sing and play instruments at a young age. As an adult, I myself am a worship leader. When life is happy, I sing. When life gets hard, I also sing. Turning on my favorite praise and worship song and singing at the top of my lungs in my kitchen can really change the atmosphere of my day. Music was the first way I was ever taught to worship. However, I needed to learn that it was neither the only nor the most important way to worship. Recently, the Holy Spirit took me on a journey of turning everything I do into worship. I changed my workout routines to be worshipful. I look at how I speak of others as worship, and I desire my conversations to be a form of worship. I fail daily to keep this mindset but I also strive to view my life as a giant ball of worship. I am still learning, and the spirit is still teaching me what it looks like to worship in spirit and in truth.

You may not like the sound of your voice, and a joyful noise to you is more stress than worship. That is not a problem. You are given opportunities to worship all day, every day, whether you realize it or not. Reading a psalm out loud and declaring it over your day can be a form of worship. How you interact with your coworker can be worship. You can merely thank the Lord for each gift you find throughout the day: the cup of coffee that wakes you up, a child that sleeps through the night, an exam that is aced. We have so many things to be thankful for. Focusing on them and whispering a "thank you Lord!" will move the heart of Christ.

Not only is worship beneficial to your relationship with Christ, but it also moves things towards victory in the spiritual realm. There is a constant battle going on for our souls. Satan does not like it when you worship the Lord, because that is one step closer to Christ and farther from him.

So he battles. He fights for your soul, because he does not want you to draw closer and dig deeper into your relationship with Christ. When you worship, you declare who your God really is and you help to win the battle for your soul. To take it one step further, you can worship for the souls of others. When they cannot battle for themselves, because life is just too hard and too heavy, you can step in and pray and worship for them.

This next week, set your minds on worshiping the Lord in more than one way. Consider doing a worship-based workout together. Put on praise and worship music while you clean the house. Set out to bring joy to someone to show that person the love of Christ. Spend a day thanking the Lord for little and big things that happen and text each other about them. I could list so many different ways that worship can happen. Be creative together. Make a list of ways that you can worship. You may just find that not only are you both focusing on the Lord and what he is doing more, but you are becoming more thankful for everything he has given you and everything he is doing in your life. He is so worthy of our praise and our worship. Set a goal to find one new way to worship each day. But do not just do it separately—worship together as a couple. That's the point of meeting together each day.

DAY 1

Scripture: 2 Chronicles 20:15, 21–22

And he said, "Listen, all Judah and inhabitants of Jerusalem and King Jehoshaphat: Thus says the Lord to you, 'Do not be afraid and do not be dismayed at this great horde, for the battle is not yours but God's'"…And when he had taken counsel with the people, he appointed those who were to sing to the Lord and praise him in holy attire, as they went before the army, and say, "Give thanks to the Lord, for his steadfast love endures forever." And when they began to sing and praise, the Lord set an ambush against the men of Ammon, Moab, and Mount Seir, who had come against Judah, so that they were routed.

DAY 1

1. God's people, led by Jehoshaphat, merely had to worship to win a war that seemed doomed. Is worship your go-to when battles seem to be raging in your life? Why or why not?

2. When it comes to worship, how comfortable are you with it? What is your definition of worship?

3. In what ways can you include more worship in your daily life?

DAY 1

Lord,

Based on the story of Jehoshaphat, we learn that worship wins battles and wars. When we worship and praise your name, things happen in the spiritual realm. The battles are not for us to carry and tackle on our own. Help us to remember that the battle is not ours, but God's, and that the Lord is always with us. When life is stressful, depressing and bleak, help us to worship. When life is full of joy, peace and happy moments, remind us to worship. May your praises be ever on our lips. You are worthy of all our time, attention, and praises. May we always praise your name in all things.

In Jesus's name,

Amen

We are grateful for...

1.

2.

3.

Prayer Requests

○

○

○

○

○

○

○

○

○

○

DAY 2

Scripture: Psalm 145:1–9

I will extol you, my God and King, and bless your name forever and ever. Every day I will bless you and praise your name forever and ever. Great is the Lord, and greatly to be praised, and his greatness is unsearchable. One generation shall commend your works to another, and shall declare your mighty acts. On the glorious splendor of your majesty, and on your wondrous works, I will meditate. They shall speak of the might of your awesome deeds, and I will declare your greatness. They shall pour forth the fame of your abundant goodness and shall sing aloud of your righteousness. The Lord is gracious and merciful, slow to anger and abounding in steadfast love. The Lord is good to all, and his mercy is over all that he has made.

DAY 2

1. Read the scripture aloud as a declaration. What emotions do the words of David evoke in you?

2. Do you find that declaring these words in worship brings forth peace, and do they remind you how great and loving our God is? Are these truths easy to forget or easy for you to hold tightly to?

3. How can these words of worship be used on a daily basis in your life?

DAY 2

Lord,

You are great and greatly to be praised! Your splendor and your majesty are beyond compare. Lord, you are gracious and merciful, slow to anger, and abounding in steadfast love. We do not deserve to be loved as well as you love us or blessed as much as you bless us. You deserve all the praise, glory, and honor. May every day of our lives be lived out singing your praises and declaring to anyone who will listen your goodness and love. Let us never forget to praise you for you are above all. No one and nothing deserves our time and attention compared to you. When words fail us, may we always utter "holy holy holy is the Lord God almighty."

In Jesus's name,

Amen

We are grateful for...

1.

2.

3.

Prayer Requests

O

O

O

O

O

O

O

O

O

O

DAY 3

Scripture: John 4:19–26

The woman said to him, "Sir, I perceive that you are a prophet. Our fathers worshiped on this mountain, but you say that in Jerusalem is the place where people ought to worship." Jesus said to her, "Woman, believe me, the hour is coming when neither on this mountain nor in Jerusalem will you worship the Father. You worship what you do not know; we worship what we know, for salvation is from the Jews. But the hour is coming, and is now here, when the true worshipers will worship the Father in spirit and truth, for the Father is seeking such people to worship him. God is spirit, and those who worship him must worship in spirit and truth." The woman said to him, "I know that Messiah is coming (he who is called Christ). When he comes, he will tell us all things." Jesus said to her, "I who speak to you am he."

DAY 3

1. Do you find yourself stuck on one way of worship and closed off to other concepts or ideas? Why or why not?

2. What does it mean to you to worship in spirit and truth? How can you apply this in your life?

3. Before Christ, worship was very ceremonial. Now we can worship whenever and wherever we want. Do you think that Christians, and possibly you personally, have taken this for granted and forgotten how to worship?

DAY 3

Lord,

Thank you that we no longer have to follow rules and guidelines to worship you. Thank you for the gift of worshiping you with not just song but with our words and actions as well. Help us to realize that all we do is considered worship when we have the right mindset. May our relationship and how we treat each other be seen as worship to you. Please bring awareness of what it means to worship you in spirit and in truth. Help us to not just understand the meaning, but to also put it into practice. May we forever be quick to sing your praises in all we do and to not take this gift lightly.

In Jesus's name,

Amen

We are grateful for…

1.

2.

3.

Prayer Requests

O

O

O

O

O

O

O

O

O

O

DAY 4

Scripture: Ephesians 5:15–21

Look carefully then how you walk, not as unwise but as wise, making the best use of the time, because the days are evil. Therefore do not be foolish, but understand what the will of the Lord is. And do not get drunk with wine, for that is debauchery, but be filled with the Spirit, addressing one another in psalms and hymns and spiritual songs, singing and making melody to the Lord with your heart, giving thanks always and for everything to God the Father in the name of our Lord Jesus Christ, submitting to one another out of reverence for Christ.

DAY 4

1. What is standing between you and true everyday worship (e.g., idols, bad habits, relationships)?

2. When you are together with fellow believers, are your words that of worship or of a more sinful nature?

3. How can you submit to each other in worship as a couple? How can you submit to your friends in worship?

DAY 4

Lord,

Today we come before you saying, "Holy Holy Holy is the Lord God almighty." We submit to worshiping you from this day forward. Remind us that when life fails us and/or words fail us, we can just come to you and repeat "Holy Holy Holy" and just those words shift something in the spiritual realm. Father, we want our relationship with those around us to be a form of worship. Please bring immediate awareness when conversations or relationships, as a whole fail to bring glory to your name. Make us aware of how we are worshiping you with our words, actions, and movements. We desire to glorify your name in all things!

In Jesus's name,

Amen

We are grateful for...

1.

2.

3.

Prayer Requests

O _____

O _____

O _____

O _____

O _____

O _____

O _____

O _____

O _____

O _____

DAY 5

Scripture: Hebrews 13:15–16, 1 Chronicles 16:8–11

Through him then let us continually offer up a sacrifice of praise to God, that is, the fruit of lips that acknowledge his name. Do not neglect to do good and to share what you have, for such sacrifices are pleasing to God. (Hebrews 13:15–16)

Oh give thanks to the Lord; call upon his name; make known his deeds among the peoples! Sing to him, sing praises to him; tell of all his wondrous works! Glory in his holy name; let the hearts of those who seek the Lord rejoice! Seek the Lord and his strength; seek his presence continually! (1 Chronicles 16:8–11)

DAY 5

1. Have you ever considered sharing the love of Christ as a form of worship? How can this concept change your daily worship life?

2. Have you already noticed your attention being drawn to worship more this week? How have you been changed?

3. Take a few minutes to put on your favorite worship song and worship together as a couple. After, discuss how this practice could change your relationship when added a few times a week?

DAY 5

Lord,

You are a faithful God. You could have given up on us time and time again. Instead, you faithfully love, protect, and guide us. Thank you for your unwavering love for us. Thank you for being patient with us as we learn to spend more time worshiping you and less time worried about ourselves and our problems. You deserve all of our time and attention. May we never lose focus on praising your name. Please help us to make worshiping you as a couple a daily part of our relationship. We want your praises to ever be on our lips. Thank you for this relationship and our time spent together with you. May we always come before you in worship together.

In Jesus's name,

Amen

We are grateful for...

1.

2.

3.

Prayer Requests

O

O

O

O

O

O

O

O

O

O

WEEK 6

Surrender

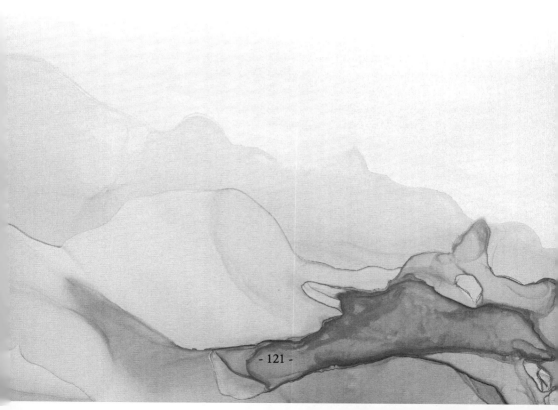

You both made it to the last week! I pray that these weeks have grown you in ways that you were not expecting, that together, you met with Jesus in a new and refreshing way, and that you both look completely different individually and as a couple. The power of prayer and spending time with Christ is a great and beautiful thing. Do not let this journey end here. Find other ways to incorporate prayer into your lives as a couple. Meditate on a scripture and memorize it together each week. Worship together as you get ready for the day. I hope this is just the beginning of your journey together.

This last week, you will focus on surrender and what that word means when applied to your life and your Christian walk. It's so very easy to walk through the day, get into a routine, and not realize that you have left out Christ. When you are not surrendering your daily life and your relationship to the leading of the Holy Spirit, it is very easy for sin to slowly creep in without you realizing it. As Christians, you must evaluate your lives daily and ask the Holy Spirit to reveal anything in your life that would be keeping you from fellowship with the Lord.

The word surrender for Christians simply means to submit to the authority of Christ. How do you need to submit to the authority of Christ in your life and in your relationship? So many want to be in control of some or all of their lives at all times. It is hard to realize that you, as a Christian, are under the authority of Christ and, whether you want to admit it or not, he knows better because he is in yesterday, today, and tomorrow at the same time. He knows you inside and out, and he recognizes how he made you and all the gifts that he has put inside of you. He sees your strengths as a couple and knows your weaknesses and your tendencies to sin. Because he knows all, you can trust that he is safe to lead and to guide you into a direction that is going to be for your good and his glory. Scripture screams of how loving and good he is. You can study the gospels and see how Christ himself went out of his way to point people in the direction of working for their good while also calling them to holiness.

Your goal should be to pattern your life after Christ and strive for holiness in all that you do. This can, and will only, be achieved by the act of surrender. This will also set up your life in a way that you are able to resist the schemes of the devil. When you surrender, you no longer look to the world and to the evil that it likes to point you toward. You focus on Christ and his holiness, and you are less likely to step into sin and sinful schemes. Daily transformation and renewal of your mind will help. But again, this can only be achieved by the workings of the Holy Spirit. It is through him that all things are possible. He was sent to this earth as a gift to help us make it through all this world wants to throw at us, and make it to the finish line of an eternity with Christ.

DAY 1

Scripture: James 4:1–8

What causes quarrels and what causes fights among you? Is it not this, that your passions are at war within you? You desire and do not have, so you murder. You covet and cannot obtain, so you fight and quarrel. You do not have, because you do not ask. You ask and do not receive, because you ask wrongly, to spend it on your passions. You adulterous people! Do you not know that friendship with the world is enmity with God? Therefore whoever wishes to be a friend of the world makes himself an enemy of God. Or do you suppose it is to no purpose that the Scripture says, "He yearns jealously over the spirit that he has made to dwell in us"? But he gives more grace. Therefore it says, "God opposes the proud but gives grace to the humble." Submit yourselves therefore to God. Resist the devil, and he will flee from you. Draw near to God, and he will draw near to you. Cleanse your hands, you sinners, and purify your hearts, you double-minded.

DAY 1

1. Where do you struggle with wanting to share friendship with the world?

2. How can you surrender these things to the Lord?

3. How can we work together to resist the devil in our personal walks and in our relationship?

DAY 1

Lord,

Thank you for being patient with us and meeting us right where we are. Thank you for not requiring perfection before we can come into your presence. Forgive us for seeking friendship with the world before coming to you first. Create in us a heart of surrender. Where we want to fit in and look appealing before the world, give us a desire for surrender to you. Point out the areas that require more of you. Help us to hold each other accountable in seeking your approval, not the approval of the world and the people around us. We desire to draw near to you, Lord. Please draw near to us and give us the weapons of defense required to resist the devil.

In Jesus's name,

Amen

We are grateful for...

1.

2.

3.

Prayer Requests

O _____

O _____

O _____

O _____

O _____

O _____

O _____

O _____

O _____

O _____

DAY 2

Scripture: Romans 12:1–2

I appeal to you therefore, brothers, by the mercies of God, to present your bodies as a living sacrifice, holy and acceptable to God, which is your spiritual worship. Do not be conformed to this world, but be transformed by the renewal of your mind, that by testing you may discern what is the will of God, what is good and acceptable and perfect.

DAY 2

1. How can you present your body as a living sacrifice in this relationship and in the world?

2. How do you see yourself trying to conform to the things of this world?

3. What does it mean to you to be transformed by the renewal of your mind? What steps can you take to start this process right away?

DAY 2

Lord,

You are good and you are gracious. You are better than anything this world has to offer. We are so quick to lose sight of this truth when the world is so quick to tempt us with the things that are seen. Help us to keep our eyes on you. We desire to be living sacrifices, holy and acceptable to you. Walk with us through the renewal of our minds on a daily basis. Show us how to test things in order to discover your will, your calling, and your direction. We do not want to look like or desire the things of this world. Continually test how we are trying to fit in, and lead our hearts to a place of daily surrender to you.

In Jesus's name,

Amen

We are grateful for...

1.

2.

3.

Prayer Requests

O

O

O

O

O

O

O

O

O

O

DAY 3

Scripture: Galatians 2:16–21

Yet we know that a person is not justified by works of the law but through faith in Jesus Christ, so we also have believed in Christ Jesus, in order to be justified by faith in Christ and not by works of the law, because by works of the law no one will be justified. But if, in our endeavor to be justified in Christ, we too were found to be sinners, is Christ then a servant of sin? Certainly not! For if I rebuild what I tore down, I prove myself to be a transgressor. For through the law I died to the law, so that I might live to God. I have been crucified with Christ. It is no longer I who live, but Christ who lives in me. And the life I now live in the flesh I live by faith in the Son of God, who loved me and gave himself for me. I do not nullify the grace of God, for if righteousness were through the law, then Christ died for no purpose.

DAY 3

1. Is it hard for you to accept that faith is all you need and works are not required to have a relationship with God? Why or why not?

2. How can you practically start dying to Christ in order to truly live? What would the first step of this process look like for you?

3. In what ways is your flesh truly holding you back from dying to Christ and living in righteousness?

DAY 3

Lord,

The world makes sin look so enticing and the thought of dying to self sounds so awful. We know your word says that we have been crucified with Christ, and it is no longer our human selves that live but Christ living and working through us. We truly desire for this to happen and for the worldly form of ourselves to no longer exist. We recognize this is a process that is never truly completed until the day we meet with you face to face. Help us to not lose hope in the process, but to run the race with endurance. We recognize that we must daily die to our worldly selves and pick up the life that we have been offered through Christ. May we hold on to you in every circumstance, and strive to mirror your image more and more every day. Thank you for the gift of a life in you.

In Jesus's name,

Amen

We are grateful for...

1.

2.

3.

Prayer Requests

○ _____

○ _____

○ _____

○ _____

○ _____

○ _____

○ _____

○ _____

○ _____

○ _____

DAY 4

Scripture: Hebrews 4:14–16, Proverbs 23:26

Since then we have a great high priest who has passed through the heavens, Jesus, the Son of God, let us hold fast our confession. For we do not have a high priest who is unable to sympathize with our weaknesses, but one who in every respect has been tempted as we are, yet without sin. Let us then with confidence draw near to the throne of grace, that we may receive mercy and find grace to help in time of need.
(Hebrews 4:14–16)

My son, give me your heart, and let your eyes observe my ways.
(Proverbs 23:26)

DAY 4

1. Is it hard for you to see Jesus as a man tempted and put through the hardships of life just like you? Why or why not?

2. How can you draw near to the throne of grace in your personal walk? Is this easy or hard for you to do?

3. What would it look like for you to fully give Christ your heart and to walk in observation of his ways?

DAY 4

Lord,

It can be so hard for us to picture you in human form being tempted the same ways that we are tempted. We see you as a holy, perfect God, and the thought that you went through what we do on a daily basis sometimes boggles our minds. But your word says you were tempted in every way and that you were able to overcome those temptations perfectly. Help us to give you our hearts fully and to observe your ways in order for us to walk in the same way that you did while you were on this earth. We know that we will not do it perfectly, the way that you did. We recognize that there will be moments of failure. But we will have your help and your guidance to overcome more than what we could on our own. Thank you for paving the way for us and showing us how to live.

In Jesus's name,

Amen

We are grateful for...

1.

2.

3.

Prayer Requests

○ _____

○ _____

○ _____

○ _____

○ _____

○ _____

○ _____

○ _____

○ _____

○ _____

DAY 5

Scripture: Psalm 37:3–7, 39–40

Trust in the Lord, and do good; dwell in the land and befriend faithfulness. Delight yourself in the Lord, and he will give you the desires of your heart. Commit your way to the Lord; trust in him, and he will act. He will bring forth your righteousness as the light, and your justice as the noonday. Be still before the Lord and wait patiently for him; fret not yourself over the one who prospers in his way, over the man who carries out evil devices! The salvation of the righteous is from the Lord; he is their stronghold in the time of trouble. The Lord helps them and delivers them; he delivers them from the wicked and saves them, because they take refuge in him.

DAY 5

1. What do you think it means to delight yourselves in the Lord?

2. Do you have trouble being still or sitting in quiet? What happens when you try to be still before the Lord?

3. How can the Lord be your stronghold from now? Are you ready to fully commit to submitting to his will for your personal life, relationship, friendships, money, and worship? How will this look from now on?

DAY 5

Lord,

You are so good to us. You are our protector, our guide, our deliverer. In you we place all of our trust. We thank you for this opportunity to spend time together growing in your word. Help us to apply the things that you have been teaching us and to fully walk in the truth of your gospel. May you ever be our stronghold in times of trouble. We ask that you help us to learn to rest in you and sit quietly at your feet. When the world gets loud and chaotic, may we find our safe space in your presence. Open our ears to hear your still, small voice so that we may be guided by you in all our comings and goings. We commit all our ways to you. We commit our relationship to you. We commit our finances and our friendships to you. May your will be done in all areas of our lives.

In Jesus's name,

Amen

We are grateful for...

1.

2.

3.

Prayer Requests

○

○

○

○

○

○

○

○

○

○

You made it to the end! You finished strong together, and I pray you continue running this race set before you. Surrender, worship, how you live your life daily, how you view your finances, and how you influence those around you are important in your daily walk. Just because you have reached the end of this particular prayer journey does not mean that you should walk away and not continually evaluate your walk in these areas individually and as a couple. Go back to these topics regularly. Read through the questions or even go through the guide again and see where you are as a couple. I pray you have set Christ on the throne of your life and relationship, and that he stays in his rightful place. Continue to journal your gratitude and your requests. Make notes on how God is answering prayers. Go back and look at what you prayed for at the beginning of this study and see how God has answered your prayers. May you find blessings upon blessings by spending time with him together! Thank you for taking this journey.